LGBTQ Debunked by Natural Law

LGBTQ Debunked by Natural Law

Kayumba David

Published by Kayumba David, 2024.

LGBTQ DEBUNKED BY NATURAL LAW

First edition. November 18, 2024.

ISBN: 979-8230193852

Written by Kayumba David.

Also by Kayumba David

1

Grow a Backbone and Walk out of an Abusive Marriage

Standalone

Cry Africa The Western Guide on How Not to Fail the Continent
Grow a Backbone and Walk out of an Abusive Marriage
Hope and Healing: A Chaplain's Handbook
Visas: The Irony of Freedom
A Meeting with Majesty: The King's Call to Humanity
Visas: The Irony of Freedom
Love Beyond Time A Comedy of Divine Connection
Silent Complicity: State Sovereignty, Global Inaction, and the Rwandan Genocide
Bridging the Rift: A Pacifist Vision for the Israel-Palestine Future
Thanks to Calvary: A Salvific Treatise on the Cross
The centuries old swindlers
Harvesting Illusions: The Global Greed and the Pan-African Paradox
Hope and Recovery - A Chaplain's Handbook
The Only Crying God in all the Universe
LGBTQ Debunked by Natural Law
The Scandal of Gentleness: Who Was Jesus?
The Day of Reckoning: Leadership, Justice, and Divine Accountability

The Greatest Woman: Every Man's Desire
The Lake of Truth
God's Interruptions

Watch for more at www.zcews.org.

Kayumba David

Preface

In the swirling tides of modern discourse, few topics spark as intense a reaction as debates surrounding LGBTQ identities and ideologies. What was once a matter of private experience and choice has become a global conversation, reaching into politics, education, religion, and the very definitions of what it means to be human. In a rapidly changing world, the foundational principles that have guided human behavior and societal cohesion for millennia are now being questioned, scrutinized, and, in some cases, discarded. *LGBTQ Irreversibly Debunked by Natural Law* seeks to explore these shifting dynamics critically. It is a call for reflection, dialogue, and a reexamination of the philosophical, historical, and moral frameworks that underpin society.

Objective of the Book

The aim of this book is not to sow division or hatred but to question the ideological foundations that have normalized and advanced LGBTQ identities within public life. Rooted in a belief that natural law is a self-evident and universal guiding principle, this work examines contemporary LGBTQ ideologies against a backdrop of millennia-old norms. Natural law, as espoused by classical thinkers such as Aristotle, Cicero, and Aquinas, asserts that human behavior and morality are inherently shaped by the natural order. This framework, which influenced centuries of human jurisprudence and societal norms, is now frequently dismissed as outdated or oppressive in modern discourse. Yet, it remains a lens through which we can interrogate the trajectory of modern culture and society.

This book's objective is clear: to engage critically with LGBTQ ideologies, their philosophical underpinnings, and societal implications, all while grounding arguments in a natural law perspective. By doing so, it aims to uncover whether contemporary movements align with or deviate from what is natural, enduring, and beneficial to humanity. It is not about denying anyone's right to exist or to live freely, but about questioning how society can best promote human flourishing through laws and norms rooted in observed natural realities.

Author's Perspective

My journey to writing this book has been shaped by personal experiences and deeply held convictions, born out of both observation and reflection. I am a product of the Global South, a region where traditional values have long been upheld, and where community and family are the bedrock of society. Growing up, I was shaped by a context that saw identity as anchored to the natural roles and responsibilities each individual bore. The modern proliferation of identities and their celebration in ways foreign to our cultural norms came as a shock, raising questions that could not easily be dismissed.

In my studies, I found solace in the writings of classical thinkers who spoke to the inherent order within nature—a universal moral code discernible through reason. Their philosophies offered a stark contrast to the relativism that dominates modern life, providing a foundation for distinguishing right from wrong, natural from unnatural. It is through this lens that I view and critique contemporary movements that seek to redefine fundamental aspects of human identity.

I recognize that my perspective may be deemed controversial, even offensive, in some quarters. Yet, I offer it not to demean or dismiss others, but to present a reasoned examination that I believe is necessary for human flourishing and societal stability. Throughout this book, I aim to be honest and direct, while acknowledging the complexity and nuance inherent in human experience.

Call for Dialogue

More than anything, this book is a call for dialogue—an earnest plea for open, respectful engagement on matters of great importance. In a world where shouting matches often replace meaningful discourse and where ideological camps rarely listen to one another, I hope to offer a bridge. My views may be strong, but my commitment to discussion is stronger still.

True progress can only come through the meeting of minds. Silencing dissenting views, as often happens in today's polarized climate, hinders humanity's growth. We cannot shy away from uncomfortable questions, nor can we assume our perspectives are infallible. We must debate, refine, and seek common ground where it can be found. If society is to thrive, we must approach contentious topics with a willingness to listen, to understand, and, where necessary, to challenge one another. This book is my contribution to that ongoing conversation—a conversation that will shape the very fabric of human society for generations to come.

Dedication

This book is dedicated to the gallant fighters in the Global South who have remained steadfast in their commitment to the principles of natural law. Your courage, resilience, and unwavering dedication to preserving timeless values inspire the quest for truth and the preservation of cultural integrity. Your efforts are a beacon of hope in a world grappling with complex challenges and shifting moral landscapes.

Table of Contents

Introduction

Definition of Natural Law

Natural law, as a concept, represents a body of unchanging moral principles regarded as a basis for all human conduct. Rooted in ancient philosophy and refined through centuries of intellectual thought, it serves as a compass for distinguishing right from wrong based on the inherent nature and order of the world. The foundation of natural law philosophy traces back to the works of Aristotle, Cicero, and later, Thomas Aquinas, who each contributed significantly to its definition and interpretation.

Aristotle laid the groundwork for natural law by positing that nature itself has a purpose, and that human beings, as rational creatures, can discern this purpose through reason. He wrote, "That which is natural is unchanging and has the same power everywhere, just as fire burns both here and in Persia" (*Nicomachean Ethics*, Book V, 1134b). For Aristotle, the essence of natural law was found in the inherent purpose and function of human beings and society. Virtue, morality, and societal harmony were linked to the fulfillment of this purpose, with deviations seen as a disruption of the natural order.

Cicero, a Roman statesman and philosopher, expanded on Aristotle's ideas, linking natural law to justice and universal morality. In *De Legibus*, he asserted, "True law is right reason in agreement with nature; it is of universal application, unchanging and everlasting; it summons to duty by its commands, and averts from wrongdoing by its prohibitions" (*De Legibus*, Book I, p. 21). Cicero emphasized that natural law transcends human laws and societal conventions; it binds all people, regardless of cultural or temporal differences, because it is derived from nature itself.

In the medieval period, Thomas Aquinas synthesized Aristotelian and Christian thought, anchoring natural law in the eternal law of God.

He described natural law as "nothing else than the rational creature's participation in the eternal law" (*Summa Theologica*, I-II, Q. 91, Art. 2). Aquinas believed that humans, endowed with reason, are capable of discerning what is good and evil by observing nature and acting in accordance with its order. For Aquinas, the natural law is immutable, and adherence to it is essential for individual and societal well-being.

Together, these thinkers provide a robust framework for understanding natural law as a set of moral principles that arise from the inherent order of nature and human reason. This framework serves as the lens through which this book examines the societal shifts and challenges presented by modern LGBTQ ideologies.

Contextualizing LGBTQ in Modern Society

The rise of LGBTQ movements in contemporary society has been marked by significant cultural, legal, and social shifts. From the Stonewall Riots in 1969 to the legal recognition of same-sex marriage in many countries, LGBTQ identities have moved from the margins to the forefront of public consciousness. This emergence is often framed as a struggle for human rights, equality, and dignity—ideals that resonate deeply in modern democratic societies.

However, this rapid normalization raises important questions about its alignment with historical and philosophical traditions rooted in natural law. Postmodernism, a philosophical movement characterized by the rejection of objective truths and embrace of subjectivity, has played a crucial role in reshaping perceptions of identity and morality. By challenging traditional norms and asserting that identity is a fluid and personal construct, postmodernism has paved the way for LGBTQ movements to gain societal acceptance and legal recognition.

Yet, this evolution has not come without controversy. Critics argue that the elevation of subjective identity over objective, observable norms undermines societal cohesion and creates tension between competing visions of morality. The notion that gender and sexual identity are socially constructed or self-determined stands in stark contrast to natural law's emphasis on an inherent, biologically grounded order.

Framing the Argument

This book seeks to explore several key questions central to the discourse on LGBTQ ideologies and their impact on society. First, is LGBTQ identity aligned with natural law as conceived by classical and medieval thinkers? If natural law asserts that morality and societal norms are rooted in the natural order, can the normalization of LGBTQ identities be reconciled with this framework, or does it represent a deviation from nature's purpose?

Second, what are the societal implications of embracing LGBTQ identities? Proponents argue that such recognition promotes inclusivity, equality, and individual freedom. However, critics contend that it disrupts traditional family structures, undermines societal stability, and challenges deeply held moral and religious beliefs. By examining these claims through the lens of natural law, this book aims to evaluate the long-term consequences for individuals, families, and communities.

Finally, the book will explore whether the rise of LGBTQ movements reflects a broader shift away from natural law and toward moral relativism, and what this means for the future of human society. In a world increasingly defined by competing ideologies, can natural law provide a unifying framework for ethical behavior and societal order? Or is it destined to be relegated to history, replaced by a more fluid and subjective moral code?

In addressing these questions, this book invites readers to engage critically and thoughtfully with one of the most pressing debates of our time. By grounding the discussion in the rich tradition of natural law philosophy, it seeks to shed light on the underlying principles and societal stakes involved, offering a perspective that emphasizes order, reason, and the common good. Whether one ultimately agrees or disagrees with its conclusions, the goal is to foster dialogue, reflection, and a deeper understanding of the forces shaping modern society.

Chapter 1

Understanding Natural Law

Historical Origins

Natural law, as a concept, represents a universal framework through which moral principles are derived from the natural world and human reason. Its historical roots trace back to the philosophies of classical thinkers, most notably Aristotle, Cicero, and later, Thomas Aquinas, who shaped and refined the doctrine to articulate the relationship between human conduct and nature's inherent order.

Aristotle, often credited with laying the groundwork for natural law theory, emphasized the idea that nature itself has an intrinsic purpose or "telos," and that humans, as rational beings, have the unique capacity to discern and fulfill this purpose. In *Nicomachean Ethics*, he wrote, "The natural is that which everywhere exists by nature and not by convention. Fire burns both here and in Persia, and similarly with all other things" (*Nicomachean Ethics*, Book V, 1134b). Aristotle saw natural law as a guide to human flourishing, which he termed "eudaimonia," achieved through living virtuously and in accordance with the rational order of nature.

Following Aristotle, Cicero, a Roman statesman and philosopher, extended the concept of natural law into the realm of universal justice. He famously declared, "True law is right reason in agreement with nature; it is of universal application, unchanging and everlasting; it summons to duty by its commands, and averts from wrongdoing by its prohibitions" (*De Legibus*, Book I, p. 21). For Cicero, natural law transcended human laws and cultural customs. It represented a universal moral code, applicable to all people at all times, because it is rooted in nature itself. Human laws, therefore, were valid only insofar as they conformed to this higher, immutable law.

In the medieval period, Thomas Aquinas synthesized Aristotelian thought with Christian theology, anchoring natural law firmly in the divine order. According to Aquinas, natural law is "nothing else than the rational creature's participation in the eternal law" (*Summa Theologica*, I-II, Q. 91, Art. 2). For Aquinas, the moral law inscribed in human nature reflects God's eternal law. He argued that humans, through reason, can discern what is good and evil, and this knowledge should guide their actions. The principles of natural law, for Aquinas, are self-evident and immutable, forming the basis for ethical behavior and legal norms. Natural law is therefore not merely a philosophical abstraction but a practical guide to living a virtuous life aligned with the order of creation.

These foundational thinkers shaped the understanding of natural law as a universal, rational, and unchanging guide for human behavior. Their insights form the basis for evaluating moral conduct and the legitimacy of human laws, a framework that has persisted for centuries.

Natural Law vs. Modern Ethical Systems

While natural law emphasizes universal principles grounded in the inherent nature of things, modern ethical systems often depart from this framework, prioritizing subjectivity, utility, and cultural context. Among the most prominent alternative ethical systems are utilitarianism and relativism, each presenting a different approach to moral reasoning.

Utilitarianism, as articulated by philosophers like Jeremy Bentham and John Stuart Mill, posits that the moral worth of an action is determined by its ability to produce the greatest happiness for the greatest number. Unlike natural law, which focuses on adherence to objective moral principles, utilitarianism is consequentialist, meaning that the morality of an action depends on its outcomes. While this approach may yield practical benefits, it can conflict with natural law's emphasis on immutable moral duties. For example, a utilitarian framework might justify actions that violate intrinsic moral principles if the outcome is perceived as beneficial for the majority. Natural law theorists argue that such reasoning undermines the stability of moral norms and the inherent dignity of the individual.

Relativism, another modern ethical system, rejects the idea of universal moral truths altogether. According to relativists, morality is shaped by cultural, historical, and personal factors, making ethical norms variable and context-dependent. In contrast to natural law's claim of universal applicability, relativism asserts that what is right or wrong depends on one's circumstances, upbringing, or cultural norms. This rejection of objective morality is antithetical to natural law's assertion that moral truths are self-evident and grounded in the natural order. As Aquinas argued, "The natural law is written in the hearts of men, for it is reason which commands them to do good and forbids them to sin" (*Summa Theologica*, I-II, Q. 94, Art. 6). Natural law theorists contend that relativism erodes moral cohesion and leads to ethical fragmentation, as it offers no firm basis for resolving moral disputes or establishing a shared moral vision for society.

Self-Evidence of Natural Law

A key claim of natural law theory is that its principles are self-evident, observable in human behavior and the natural world. This idea stems from the belief that nature itself reveals a moral order, accessible through human reason. Aquinas, for instance, argued that the basic precepts of natural law—such as the pursuit of good and avoidance of evil—are "self-evident to human beings" (*Summa Theologica*, I-II, Q. 94, Art. 2). This self-evidence is demonstrated through the natural inclinations of humans to seek knowledge, form communities, and reproduce, all of which reflect the order inherent in human nature.

The self-evidence of natural law is supported by observable patterns in human behavior and societal norms. For example, the concept of justice—treating others fairly and fulfilling one's obligations—has been recognized and valued across diverse cultures and historical periods. Such universality suggests that there is a common moral law rooted in the nature of human beings. As Cicero wrote, "There is in fact a true law—namely, right reason—which is in accordance with nature, applies to all men, and is unchangeable and eternal" (*De Legibus*, Book I, p. 23).

Critics of natural law may challenge its claim to self-evidence, pointing to cultural and moral diversity as evidence of moral relativism. However, proponents argue that deviations from natural law often result from ignorance, flawed reasoning, or the influence of corrupt customs, rather than a rejection of its inherent validity. As Aquinas observed, "Even though humans may diverge from the dictates of reason, this does not mean that the law itself is not clear and evident" (*Summa Theologica*, I-II, Q. 94, Art. 4).

In sum, natural law is presented as an immutable moral code, grounded in the nature of reality and accessible through human reason. It stands in contrast to modern ethical systems that prioritize subjective judgments and variable outcomes. By grounding moral behavior in what is perceived as a universal, self-evident order, natural law offers a framework for evaluating human actions and societal norms in a consistent and enduring manner. This foundational understanding is essential for addressing the complex moral and societal challenges posed by contemporary movements and ideologies.

Chapter 2

The Unchangeable Order of Nature

Biological Foundations of Gender and Sexuality

The biological foundations of gender and sexuality are rooted in the observable, complementary roles of male and female in human reproduction and society. Across cultures and throughout history, this binary complementarity has been central to human existence, providing a stable framework for family formation and societal continuity. Classical natural law thinkers, who emphasize the inherent purpose of natural phenomena, argue that this complementarity is self-evident and reflects a natural order that should be preserved.

Aristotle, for instance, saw human beings as "political animals" who are naturally inclined toward social bonds that fulfill specific functions, such as reproduction and child-rearing. In *Politics,* he stated, "The male is by nature superior, and the female inferior; and the one rules, and the other is ruled" (Book I, 1254b). While this perspective may reflect historical biases, it underscores the perceived necessity of gender roles in fulfilling what Aristotle viewed as nature's purpose. The biological complementarity between male and female is seen as the bedrock of societal order and human flourishing.

Thomas Aquinas built upon this view by integrating Aristotelian philosophy with Christian theology. He argued that the union of male and female in marriage is "ordered to the procreation and upbringing of children," which is both natural and necessary for the continuation of society (*Summa Theologica,* I-II, Q. 94, Art. 2). For Aquinas, this complementarity is not merely a biological fact but a moral imperative rooted in the natural law. The roles of male and female, and their union within the context of marriage, reflect a divinely ordained order that promotes human flourishing and societal stability.

Nature's Observable Patterns

In nature, patterns of behavior among animal species often reflect a clear order and structure that contributes to the survival and well-being of the species. From mating rituals to parenting behaviors, the natural world exhibits an observable order that serves as a model for human norms. Natural law theorists argue that human beings, as rational creatures, are called to reflect and build upon these natural patterns rather than subvert them.

For example, many species exhibit behaviors that promote the stability and survival of their communities. The role differentiation between male and female animals often revolves around reproductive and nurturing functions, ensuring that offspring are protected and raised in a stable environment. These natural behaviors align with the human institution of the family, wherein the complementary roles of men and women contribute to the well-being of children and the stability of society.

Critics of natural law may point out instances of same-sex behavior in certain animal species as evidence that such behaviors are natural. However, proponents counter that such instances are exceptions rather than the rule and do not reflect the normative purpose of reproduction and family formation. As Aquinas noted, "Everything acts for the sake of an end, and this is evident from their acting always, or nearly always, in the same way, so as to obtain the best result" (*Summa Contra Gentiles*, Book III, Chapter 2). From this perspective, behaviors that deviate from the natural order are seen as anomalies rather than norms to be emulated.

Natural Family Structures

The traditional family structure, characterized by the union of a male and female and their roles in raising children, has long been regarded as a cornerstone of societal stability. Natural law theorists argue that the family is not a social construct subject to redefinition but a natural institution grounded in the biological and moral complementarity of the sexes.

Studies on family structures have consistently highlighted the benefits of stable, two-parent households for children's well-being. Research by sociologist Sara McLanahan and others has shown that children raised in intact families generally fare better in terms of educational attainment, mental health, and social behavior than those raised in fragmented family structures (McLanahan & Sandefur, *Growing Up with a Single Parent: What Hurts, What Helps*, 1994, p. 53). Proponents of natural law view these findings as evidence of nature's unchanging order and the importance of preserving traditional family roles.

The erosion of these roles, natural law advocates argue, has significant consequences for societal stability. Rising rates of divorce, single parenthood, and alternative family structures are often cited as contributing factors to various social issues, including poverty, crime, and mental health challenges. Cicero's assertion that "the stability of human society rests upon the sanctity of marriage and the preservation of family" (*De Officiis*, Book I, p. 127) resonates with those who see the traditional family as essential to social cohesion and the moral upbringing of future generations.

Underhand Methods and Global Pressures

In contemporary debates, critics of LGBTQ advocacy in the Global South often argue that such movements are not purely organic but are driven, at least in part, by external influences and pressures. International organizations, NGOs, and some Western governments have been accused of using conditional aid and economic incentives to promote acceptance of LGBTQ rights in countries with deeply rooted traditional values. These actions are viewed as forms of cultural imperialism, whereby Western norms are imposed on societies that have long adhered to natural law principles.

This phenomenon raises ethical questions about the methods used to promote LGBTQ rights and the potential for coercion. For example, the tying of foreign aid to the adoption of LGBTQ-friendly policies has been criticized as an attempt to undermine local cultures and impose a foreign moral framework. Critics argue that such tactics are a form of moral and cultural coercion that disrupts the natural order and societal norms of the Global South.

In summary, the unchangeable order of nature, as articulated by natural law, emphasizes the biological complementarity of male and female, the observable patterns of behavior in nature, and the stability provided by traditional family structures. These principles, proponents argue, are under threat from modern ideologies and external pressures that seek to redefine fundamental aspects of human identity and society. By upholding the natural order, societies can promote stability, continuity, and human flourishing, while resisting efforts to subvert their cultural and moral foundations.

Chapter 3

LGBTQ: A Postmodern Invention

Postmodernism and Its Influence

Postmodernism, a philosophical movement that rose to prominence in the mid-20th century, fundamentally challenges the notion of absolute truths, objective morality, and fixed social norms. This paradigm shift has had a profound influence on contemporary discussions around identity, morality, and social constructs, laying much of the groundwork for the normalization of LGBTQ identities within society. The postmodern emphasis on deconstructing established norms and embracing subjective interpretations of reality has driven a reevaluation of traditional moral and social frameworks, including those rooted in natural law.

Thinkers such as Michel Foucault argued that sexuality, like other aspects of human behavior, is a social construct shaped by historical and cultural power dynamics. In *The History of Sexuality*, Foucault wrote, "Sexuality must not be thought of as a kind of natural given which power tries to hold in check... It is the name that can be given to a historical construct" (Foucault, 1978, p. 105). From this perspective, categories such as heterosexuality and homosexuality are seen as products of cultural discourse rather than immutable aspects of human nature. This stance challenges the natural law tradition, which views human sexuality as a reflection of a divinely or naturally ordained order.

Natural law theorists, including classical thinkers like Aristotle and medieval philosophers such as Thomas Aquinas, have long argued for the existence of a universal moral code grounded in the natural order of creation. For these thinkers, human beings possess an intrinsic nature and purpose that can be discerned through reason. Aristotle asserted that "by nature, living beings are differentiated into male and female, and this differentiation serves the purpose of reproduction" (*Politics*, Book I, 1253a). The idea that human beings should live in accordance with their natural purpose stands in stark contrast to postmodern ideas of fluidity and the rejection of fixed norms.

Subjective Identity vs. Objective Reality

At the heart of the clash between LGBTQ ideologies and natural law is the conflict between subjective identity and objective reality. LGBTQ movements often emphasize the right of individuals to define their own identities, regardless of biological or societal norms. This focus on self-determination and fluidity is in line with postmodern thought, which seeks to deconstruct rigid categories and challenge traditional hierarchies.

In contrast, natural law philosophy posits that human identity and moral obligations are rooted in the natural order. Thomas Aquinas argued that "the natural law is nothing else than the participation of the eternal law in the rational creature" (*Summa Theologica*, I-II, Q. 91, Art. 2). According to this view, human beings are unique among creatures because of their capacity for reason, which allows them to discern and act in accordance with natural law. This rational capacity is what sets humans apart from animals and underpins the moral and legal systems that hold individuals accountable for their actions.

The significance of rationality as a defining characteristic of human beings becomes evident when we consider the distinction between human actions and the actions of animals. For instance, a human being who commits murder is held accountable and faces moral and legal consequences. In contrast, a lion that kills a human being is not morally culpable; it acts according to its instincts and the laws of nature. The difference lies in the human capacity for rationality and moral agency, which, according to natural law, imposes a duty to act in accordance with what is good and just. As Aquinas noted, "It is proper to man to act according to reason" (*Summa Theologica*, I-II, Q. 94, Art. 3). If natural law were wrong or non-existent, the very basis for holding humans morally accountable would be called into question. Without an objective moral framework, concepts of justice, accountability, and ethical behavior would become subjective and arbitrary.

Role of Media and Academia

The media and academia have played a significant role in shaping public perceptions of LGBTQ identities and promoting the idea that gender and sexuality are fluid constructs. Through films, television, literature, and scholarly work, these institutions have normalized LGBTQ narratives and framed them as integral to modern conceptions of freedom, equality, and self-expression. This cultural influence is often viewed by proponents of natural law as a deliberate attempt to reshape societal norms and undermine traditional values.

Media portrayals of LGBTQ individuals frequently emphasize themes of courage, authenticity, and victimhood, creating a powerful narrative that resonates with many people. While representation can be empowering for marginalized groups, critics argue that these portrayals often ignore the complexities and philosophical implications of redefining gender and sexuality. Philosopher Roger Scruton highlighted the role of media in shaping perceptions when he wrote, "The power of the image in modern media does not merely reflect reality but creates it" (*The Uses of Pessimism*, p. 45). By framing LGBTQ identities in a particular light, media narratives can shape societal attitudes and marginalize dissenting viewpoints, often casting traditional beliefs as outdated or oppressive.

Academia, particularly within the fields of gender studies and queer theory, has provided the intellectual foundation for challenging traditional norms around gender and sexuality. The emphasis on deconstructing categories and promoting fluidity aligns with postmodern thought but stands in opposition to the natural law tradition. Critics argue that this academic focus often leads to ideological conformity, stifling genuine debate and marginalizing scholars who question or critique LGBTQ narratives. Jürgen Habermas, a philosopher known for his critique of modernity, warned against the "colonization of the lifeworld," in which dominant ideologies shape public perception and suppress alternative viewpoints (*The Theory of Communicative Action*, p. 366).

Underhand Methods and the Global South

Critics of the global promotion of LGBTQ rights often point to what they perceive as underhand methods used by Western governments, NGOs, and international organizations to influence cultural and legal norms in the Global South. These methods include tying foreign aid to the adoption of LGBTQ-friendly policies, exerting diplomatic pressure, and leveraging economic incentives to reshape traditional values. Such tactics are viewed by many as a form of cultural imperialism that disregards the unique moral, religious, and cultural contexts of these societies.

For example, numerous countries in Africa and the Middle East have faced international pressure to decriminalize homosexuality or adopt policies that promote LGBTQ rights. While proponents of these efforts argue that they are necessary for the protection of human rights, critics contend that they impose a foreign moral framework on societies that have historically adhered to natural law principles. As Cicero observed, "To disregard the customs and laws of one's own nation is a violation of nature" (*De Republica*, Book III, p. 45). From this perspective, efforts to promote LGBTQ rights through coercion or manipulation are seen as an affront to cultural sovereignty and an attempt to subvert the natural order.

In conclusion, the rise of LGBTQ ideologies, driven in part by postmodernist thought, presents a fundamental challenge to traditional notions of identity, morality, and social order rooted in natural law. The conflict between subjective identity and objective reality, coupled with the influence of media, academia, and international pressures, highlights the complex and often contentious nature of this cultural shift. By examining these issues through the lens of natural law, this chapter seeks to illuminate the broader philosophical, social, and cultural implications of the LGBTQ movement and its impact on society.

The LGBTQ movement, with its focus on redefining gender, sexuality, and identity, represents one of the most significant cultural shifts of modern times. Its emergence has broad philosophical, social, and cultural implications that extend far beyond questions of personal freedom or individual rights. By challenging long-established norms and introducing new frameworks for understanding human identity and relationships, the LGBTQ movement compels societies to reevaluate core values, ethical principles, and social structures. Here, I will illuminate the broader implications of this movement through the lenses of philosophy, society, and culture.

Philosophical Implications

1. Subjectivity vs. Objectivity

At the heart of the LGBTQ movement lies a tension between subjective self-identification and the objective frameworks traditionally used to understand human nature and morality. The assertion that gender and sexuality are fluid and subject to individual choice challenges longstanding beliefs about the immutable aspects of human identity. In the past, gender and sexuality were largely viewed through the lens of natural law, which posited that human behavior should conform to the natural order discernible through reason. Philosophers such as Thomas

Aquinas argued that human beings are bound by a moral code rooted in this natural order, which serves as a guide for ethical conduct and social norms (*Summa Theologica*, I-II, Q. 94, Art. 2).

By contrast, the LGBTQ movement, influenced by postmodernist philosophy, emphasizes the fluidity and socially constructed nature of identity. This perspective suggests that individuals have the right to define themselves in ways that may not align with traditional categories or biological realities. While this view promotes autonomy and self-expression, it also raises philosophical questions about the nature of identity and morality. If identity is purely subjective, what becomes of shared moral principles and societal norms? Can a society function cohesively without a common understanding of human nature and purpose? These are critical questions that continue to shape philosophical debates around gender, sexuality, and identity.

2. Deconstruction of Norms

The LGBTQ movement's emphasis on challenging and deconstructing traditional norms reflects the influence of postmodernist thought, which seeks to destabilize established power structures and reveal the cultural biases underpinning them. Michel Foucault, a key figure in this intellectual movement, argued that concepts such as sexuality are shaped by power relations and cultural discourse rather than by any inherent or universal truths (*The History of Sexuality*, 1978). While this approach has led to greater awareness of marginalized identities and experiences, it also invites philosophical challenges regarding the role of norms and traditions in fostering social cohesion and ethical behavior.

Traditionalists argue that norms rooted in natural law or religious teachings provide a stable moral framework that guides behavior and promotes human flourishing. When these norms are deconstructed or dismissed, they contend, society risks descending into moral relativism, where there are no objective standards for judging right and wrong.

This philosophical tension between deconstruction and moral tradition lies at the core of contemporary debates about the implications of the LGBTQ movement.

Social Implications

1. Redefinition of Family Structures

The LGBTQ movement has played a pivotal role in redefining family structures, challenging the traditional model of a family as consisting of a heterosexual couple and their biological children. Same-sex marriages, parenting by LGBTQ individuals, and diverse family arrangements are now legally recognized in many countries, reflecting broader social acceptance of alternative family structures.

While proponents argue that these changes promote inclusivity and recognize the legitimacy of diverse relationships, critics raise concerns about their potential impact on societal stability. Research has shown that children raised in stable, two-parent households often fare better in terms of educational outcomes, mental health, and social behavior (McLanahan & Sandefur, *Growing Up with a Single Parent: What Hurts, What Helps*, 1994). Traditionalists argue that the biological complementarity of male and female parents plays a unique role in child development and that redefining family structures may have unforeseen social consequences. However, supporters of LGBTQ rights emphasize that stability, love, and support within a family are more important than its composition.

2. Legal and Political Shifts

The growing recognition of LGBTQ rights has led to significant legal and political changes around the world, including the legalization of same-sex marriage, anti-discrimination protections, and gender identity recognition laws. These legal shifts reflect evolving social norms and aim to promote equality and protect the rights of LGBTQ individuals. However, they have also sparked backlash in many societies, particularly those with strong religious or traditionalist values.

The legal recognition of LGBTQ rights raises important questions about the limits of personal freedom and the role of the state in shaping social norms. Should the state have the authority to redefine marriage, gender, and other fundamental aspects of human identity? What happens when the legal recognition of one group's rights conflicts with the religious or moral beliefs of others? These questions highlight the complex social and political dynamics surrounding the LGBTQ movement and its impact on society.

Cultural Implications

1. Cultural Imperialism and the Global South

One of the most contentious aspects of the LGBTQ movement's global impact is the perception that Western countries and international organizations are imposing LGBTQ-friendly policies on cultures with deeply rooted traditional values. Critics argue that efforts to promote LGBTQ rights in the Global South often involve economic incentives, diplomatic pressure, and conditional aid, amounting to a form of cultural imperialism. While proponents of these efforts frame them as necessary for the protection of human rights, critics see them as an attempt to impose foreign values on culturally sovereign societies.

This cultural clash raises questions about the ethics of promoting LGBTQ rights globally. Is it legitimate to use economic leverage to influence cultural norms? What role should international organizations play in shaping the moral and cultural frameworks of diverse societies? For many in the Global South, the promotion of LGBTQ rights by external actors is seen as a challenge to their cultural, religious, and moral traditions, leading to tensions and resistance.

2. Influence of Media and Cultural Narratives

Media and popular culture have played a crucial role in shaping public perceptions of LGBTQ identities and promoting their normalization. Through films, television, literature, and social media, LGBTQ characters and narratives have become increasingly visible, contributing to greater awareness and acceptance. While representation is important for challenging stereotypes and fostering inclusivity, critics argue that media portrayals often present a one-sided view of LGBTQ issues, marginalizing traditional beliefs and framing dissenting voices as bigoted or intolerant.

The power of cultural narratives to shape societal norms and values cannot be underestimated. Philosopher Roger Scruton noted, "The media creates its own reality by selecting and presenting facts that conform to a narrative" (*The Uses of Pessimism*, p. 45). In the context of LGBTQ representation, media narratives often reflect and reinforce specific cultural values, influencing public attitudes and shaping the terms of public debate. This cultural influence has significant implications for how societies understand gender, sexuality, and identity, often leading to tensions between progressivism and tradition.

Conclusion

The LGBTQ movement's impact on society is far-reaching, encompassing philosophical, social, and cultural dimensions that challenge traditional norms and reshape modern life. By promoting subjective self-identification, redefining family structures, and influencing legal and cultural norms, the movement compels societies to confront difficult questions about identity, morality, and social cohesion. While proponents view these changes as necessary for promoting equality and individual freedom, critics warn of the potential consequences for societal stability, moral order, and cultural sovereignty. As society grapples with these complex issues, it is essential to foster open, respectful dialogue that allows for diverse perspectives and thoughtful consideration of the broader implications of this transformative cultural shift.

Chapter 4

Historical Rejection of Homosexual Practices

Ancient Civilizations and LGBTQ Practices

Throughout history, societies have approached same-sex practices with a range of responses, often shaped by cultural norms, social structures, and philosophical beliefs. These responses provide insight into the longstanding tension between traditional values and individual expressions of sexuality.

In Ancient Greece, same-sex relationships were present and, in some contexts, even celebrated. The practice of pederasty—relationships between adult men and adolescent boys—was a notable part of Greek aristocratic life, particularly in educational and military settings. However, this practice operated within strict social boundaries, and same-sex relationships were generally seen as secondary to the heterosexual family unit, which was vital for procreation and societal continuity. Plato, in his later work *Laws*, expressed concern about the moral and societal implications of same-sex relationships, emphasizing the primacy of procreative unions: "It is a disgrace for men to have intercourse with men or to have intercourse contrary to nature" (*Laws*, Book VIII, 836a).

In Ancient Rome, attitudes toward homosexuality were more complex and often linked to power dynamics and notions of masculinity. While same-sex relationships were tolerated, they were regulated by social norms that emphasized dominance and status. Roman citizens, particularly men of high standing, were expected to assert their dominance in sexual relations, while assuming a passive role was seen as shameful. As the Roman Empire transitioned to Christian influence, official attitudes toward homosexuality became more rigid, with increasing condemnation and legal prohibitions. The Justinian Code, for example, prescribed severe penalties for same-sex acts, framing them as "unnatural" and a threat to divine and societal order.

Religious Doctrines

The major religious traditions, including Christianity, Islam, and traditional African beliefs, have historically condemned homosexual practices as inconsistent with moral and natural law.

Christianity: The Christian tradition has consistently viewed homosexual behavior as contrary to the moral law established by God. Biblical passages such as Leviticus 18:22 explicitly prohibit same-sex relations: "You shall not lie with a male as with a woman; it is an abomination." The New Testament also reiterates this stance, with the Apostle Paul condemning same-sex acts as evidence of moral corruption in Romans 1:27. Early Church Fathers, including Augustine and later Thomas Aquinas, emphasized that sexual acts must be ordered toward procreation and that any deviation from this purpose was morally reprehensible. Aquinas wrote in *Summa Theologica* that "the unnatural vice is a species of lust that is especially grave because it goes against the natural order of the act" (*Summa Theologica*, II-II, Q. 154, Art. 11).

Islam: Islamic teachings, rooted in the Quran and Hadith, similarly view homosexual acts as forbidden (haram). The story of the people of Lot, who were punished by God for engaging in same-sex relations, serves as a clear indication of divine disapproval (Quran 7:80-84). Islamic jurisprudence has historically prescribed severe penalties for such acts, emphasizing that they violate both natural and divine law. Medieval Islamic scholars, including Ibn Kathir, noted that homosexual acts were considered "unnatural, against the innate disposition, and contrary to the intentions of Allah" (*Tafsir Ibn Kathir*, Vol. 3).

Traditional African Beliefs: In many traditional African societies, gender and sexual roles were rooted in cultural and spiritual norms that emphasized procreation, family continuity, and communal well-being. Homosexuality was often viewed as a deviation from these roles, with social sanctions ranging from ostracism to punishment. Anthropologist E.E. Evans-Pritchard documented that among the Nuer people, for example, any deviation from accepted sexual norms was met with resistance, as it threatened the social fabric and community harmony (*The Nuer: A Description of the Modes of Livelihood and Political Institutions of a Nilotic People*, 1940).

Colonial Legacy and Laws

The colonial period had a profound impact on the legal regulation of homosexuality in many parts of the world, including Africa, Asia, and the Caribbean. European colonial powers, particularly the British Empire, introduced laws that criminalized same-sex relations, often using Victorian-era moral standards as their justification. These laws remain influential in many former colonies today, shaping contemporary attitudes toward LGBTQ identities and practices.

In Uganda, the British colonialists enacted laws that specifically punished same-sex relations. Section 145 of the Penal Code, introduced during the colonial era, criminalized "carnal knowledge against the order of nature," a vague and broad term used to target homosexual acts. This law, reflecting the moral and legal standards of the time, was intended to enforce what the British considered proper social behavior. Despite Uganda's independence, this colonial-era law has remained in the country's penal code and continues to influence public and legal attitudes toward homosexuality. The persistence of such laws is often framed by proponents as a defense of traditional values, while critics argue that they reflect the lingering influence of colonial rule and serve to marginalize LGBTQ individuals.

The colonial legacy of anti-sodomy laws highlights the complex interplay between historical, cultural, and legal factors in shaping contemporary attitudes toward homosexuality. While many countries have moved toward repealing or reforming these laws, others have resisted, framing the debate as a struggle between traditional values and perceived foreign influence. This tension underscores the broader challenges of reconciling historical legacies with evolving social norms and human rights discourses.

In conclusion, the historical rejection of homosexual practices by ancient civilizations, religious traditions, and colonial-era legal frameworks provides critical context for contemporary debates around LGBTQ rights and identities. By examining these historical perspectives, we gain a deeper understanding of the cultural, religious, and legal factors that continue to shape societal attitudes toward homosexuality. Whether viewed as a reflection of natural law, religious doctrine, or colonial influence, these historical responses offer valuable insights into the complex dynamics of gender, sexuality, and human morality.

Chapter 5

The Philosophical Pitfalls of LGBTQ Ideology

Logical Inconsistencies

One of the most significant criticisms of contemporary LGBTQ ideology centers on perceived logical inconsistencies that challenge its internal coherence and broader social messaging. Central to LGBTQ activism is the notion that gender and sexuality are fluid and can be self-determined, independent of biological realities. This belief emphasizes personal autonomy and rejects traditional norms rooted in biological sex differences. However, this perspective often runs into contradictions when it demands rigid legal recognition and societal accommodation for these self-identified categories.

Natural law, as articulated by thinkers such as Aristotle and Aquinas, asserts that human beings have a defined nature and purpose that can be discerned through reason and is grounded in biological realities. Aristotle observed, "Nature makes nothing in vain, and man's nature is discernible by his ends and purposes" (*Politics*, Book I, 1252b). For natural law theorists, the essence of human identity is tied to the biological and moral order, making any self-determined deviation inherently problematic. This perspective challenges the idea that subjective identity can supersede objective reality without creating contradictions.

The inconsistency becomes apparent when the fluidity of gender and sexuality, a foundational concept within LGBTQ activism, demands immutable legal recognition, such as the enforcement of specific pronouns, legal categories for gender identity, and accommodations in public spaces. If gender and sexuality are fluid, how can they be legislatively fixed or protected in a rigid manner? Such contradictions, critics argue, weaken the ideological coherence of LGBTQ advocacy. Furthermore, whatever defies natural law and reason based on biological science and has to be pushed into society with "choking and deafening screams"—through public pressure, media campaigns, and institutional enforcement—cannot be entirely right. The need for coercive measures suggests an inherent fragility in the arguments being advanced.

The Role of Identity Politics

Identity politics has become a driving force in LGBTQ activism, seeking to elevate the experiences and perspectives of marginalized groups by emphasizing the unique struggles associated with their identities. While this approach has been effective in raising awareness and advancing legal protections, it has also been criticized for creating societal fragmentation and for fostering a culture of division rather than unity.

Roger Scruton, a conservative philosopher, highlighted the divisive nature of identity politics, noting that "The politics of identity is a politics of division, a politics that leads people to define themselves against others rather than in terms of shared goals and common values" (*Fools, Frauds and Firebrands: Thinkers of the New Left*, p. 213). By focusing on individual identity categories, identity politics risks pitting different groups against each other and undermining social cohesion. This can result in a zero-sum game, where one group's gains are perceived as another's losses, fostering resentment and polarization.

From the perspective of natural law, which emphasizes the common good and the moral order rooted in human nature, identity politics can be seen as a deviation from the pursuit of shared societal goals. Aristotle argued that "the good of the city is more important than the good of the individual" (*Politics*, Book III, 1278b). Identity politics, by contrast, elevates individual self-expression and group identity over collective values, potentially eroding the bonds that hold communities together. When LGBTQ activism relies on identity politics, it risks marginalizing those who adhere to traditional norms and creating divisions that weaken the fabric of society.

Freedom of Expression vs. Silencing Dissent

One of the central contradictions within LGBTQ activism is its treatment of freedom of expression and dissenting views. While the movement often frames itself as a champion of inclusivity and diversity, it has been criticized for silencing or marginalizing voices that challenge its premises. This paradox is evident in the way dissenting perspectives on gender and sexuality are often labeled as "hate speech" or dismissed as bigotry, effectively stifling genuine debate and open discourse.

John Stuart Mill, in his seminal work *On Liberty*, argued for the necessity of free and open debate, stating, "The peculiar evil of silencing the expression of an opinion is that it robs the human race... If the opinion is right, they are deprived of the opportunity of exchanging error for truth; if wrong, they lose, what is almost as great a benefit, the clearer perception and livelier impression of truth, produced by its collision with error" (*On Liberty*, Chapter 2). Mill's warning is especially relevant in contemporary discussions around LGBTQ issues, where dissenting views are often met with harsh censure rather than reasoned engagement.

The phenomenon of "cancel culture" exemplifies the challenges posed by the suppression of dissent. Public figures, academics, and ordinary citizens who express views contrary to LGBTQ orthodoxy may face social ostracism, professional consequences, or even threats. Critics argue that this stifling of debate is antithetical to the principles of free expression and mutual respect that are essential for a pluralistic society. When ideas are advanced through coercive tactics, "choking and deafening screams," and institutional force, it raises questions about the legitimacy and resilience of the arguments themselves. If an idea cannot withstand scrutiny, proponents often resort to silencing opposition—a tactic that suggests inherent weaknesses.

Scholarly Perspectives on Free Speech and Identity Movements

The relationship between free speech and identity politics has been the subject of intense scholarly debate. Jürgen Habermas, a German philosopher and sociologist, warned of the dangers posed by the "colonization of the lifeworld," wherein dominant ideologies seek to control public discourse and marginalize opposing viewpoints (*The Theory of Communicative Action*, p. 366). When identity movements, including LGBTQ activism, dominate the narrative and suppress dissent, they risk alienating those who hold different perspectives and creating a climate of conformity and fear.

The challenge for society is to strike a balance between protecting the rights of marginalized groups and preserving the space for free and open debate. While it is essential to protect individuals from discrimination and violence, it is equally important to ensure that public discourse remains a forum for the exchange of diverse ideas and perspectives. Suppressing dissent may achieve short-term gains, but it ultimately undermines the credibility of any movement and weakens the foundations of a free and democratic society.

Conclusion

The philosophical pitfalls of LGBTQ ideology, including its logical inconsistencies, reliance on identity politics, and approach to freedom of expression, reveal deeper tensions within contemporary society. By examining these issues critically, we gain a better understanding of the complex dynamics at play and the challenges of balancing individual autonomy with collective norms. Whether viewed as a force for progress or a source of division, the LGBTQ movement raises important questions about the nature of identity, morality, and social cohesion. It is through open dialogue, reasoned debate, and a commitment to truth that society can navigate these challenges and seek a path toward genuine understanding and mutual respect.

Chapter 6

The Societal Impact of Disrupting Natural Law

Family and Community Fragmentation

The traditional family structure, rooted in the complementary roles of men and women and oriented toward the upbringing of children, has historically been considered the cornerstone of societal stability and well-being. Proponents of natural law argue that the disruption of these natural norms, whether through the redefinition of marriage, the normalization of non-reproductive unions, or the rejection of traditional gender roles, leads to fragmentation within families and communities. This fragmentation, in turn, has significant consequences for societal cohesion and individual flourishing.

The classical thinkers who shaped the foundation of natural law were deeply aware of the importance of the family as the primary unit of social organization. Aristotle, in his *Politics*, described the family as "the association established by nature for the supply of men's everyday wants" and emphasized that "the family is the first and most essential cell of human society" (Book I, 1253b). For Aristotle, the family was the building block upon which the polis (city-state) rested, and its stability was essential for the well-being of the larger community.

The disruption of traditional family structures has been linked to a range of social problems, including poverty, crime, and decreased educational outcomes. Studies have consistently shown that children raised in stable, two-parent households tend to fare better than those from fragmented or single-parent families. According to sociologist Sara McLanahan, "Children who grow up with only one biological parent are worse off, on average, than children who grow up with both parents in terms of educational attainment, social behavior, and mental health"

(*Growing Up with a Single Parent: What Hurts, What Helps*, 1994, p. 53). This evidence supports the view that adherence to natural norms regarding family structure promotes societal stability and individual well-being.

From a natural law perspective, the breakdown of traditional family roles and the normalization of alternative family structures are seen as deviations from the natural order. Thomas Aquinas emphasized that "marriage is by its nature ordered to the procreation and education of offspring" and that deviations from this purpose disrupt the harmony and stability of human society (*Summa Theologica*, II-II, Q. 154, Art. 2). When family structures are weakened, communities become more fragmented, and the bonds that hold society together begin to fray.

Mental Health Implications

The impact of disrupting natural norms extends beyond family and community fragmentation; it also has profound implications for individual mental health and identity formation. Research has shown that stable family environments, rooted in clear gender roles and traditional values, contribute to the mental and emotional well-being of children and adults. Conversely, the erosion of these norms and the embrace of fluid or non-traditional identities can lead to increased rates of mental health issues, including anxiety, depression, and identity confusion.

A 2019 study published in the *Journal of the American Medical Association* (JAMA) found that LGBTQ youth are at a significantly higher risk of experiencing mental health challenges, including depression and suicidal ideation, compared to their heterosexual peers (Haas et al., *JAMA Pediatrics*, 2019). While some attribute these disparities to societal stigma and discrimination, others argue that they may also reflect the inherent psychological challenges of navigating fluid and often contested identities. The rejection of natural law principles and traditional norms can create a sense of disorientation and instability, contributing to mental health struggles.

Philosopher Alasdair MacIntyre, in his critique of modern moral relativism, argued that the absence of a stable moral framework leads to a sense of "moral fragmentation" and existential crisis (*After Virtue*, p. 204). For MacIntyre, the erosion of traditional norms, including those related to family and gender, creates a moral vacuum that leaves individuals struggling to find meaning and purpose. This observation aligns with the experiences of many individuals who grapple with identity formation in a society that increasingly rejects fixed norms and values.

Statistical Evidence

Empirical studies on family structure and societal health provide additional support for the argument that adherence to natural norms is essential for societal well-being. Numerous studies have demonstrated the correlation between stable family environments and positive outcomes for children, including academic achievement, mental health, and social behavior. For example, a 2015 study by the Brookings Institution found that children raised in intact, two-parent families were more likely to succeed academically, avoid criminal behavior, and achieve economic stability in adulthood (Wilcox et al., *The Family and Economic Success*, 2015).

Data from the National Longitudinal Survey of Youth (NLSY) similarly highlight the importance of family stability. Children from stable, married households are less likely to experience poverty, substance abuse, and mental health issues compared to children from single-parent or cohabiting households (McLanahan & Sandefur, *Growing Up with a Single Parent*, 1994). These findings reinforce the argument that the natural family structure, rooted in the complementarity of male and female roles, plays a crucial role in promoting societal stability and individual well-being.

In contrast, the normalization of alternative family structures and the rejection of traditional gender roles have been linked to negative social outcomes. The rise of single-parent households, cohabitation, and same-sex parenting has introduced new challenges for policymakers, educators, and social workers. While proponents of these changes argue that love and commitment, rather than family structure, are the most important factors for child well-being, critics maintain that empirical evidence supports the unique benefits of traditional family arrangements.

Scholarly Reference: Empirical Studies on Family Structure and Societal Health

The body of scholarly work on family structure and its impact on societal health is extensive. Sociologists, psychologists, and economists have all contributed to our understanding of the importance of stable family environments. For example, a study by Paul Amato in *Journal of Marriage and Family* found that "children from stable, two-parent families are more likely to have better physical and mental health, higher academic achievement, and more positive social behaviors than those from unstable or non-traditional families" (Amato, 2005, p. 945). This research underscores the importance of adhering to natural norms regarding family structure and the potential consequences of deviating from these norms.

Conclusion

The societal impact of disrupting natural law extends far beyond individual experiences; it affects the stability and cohesion of families, communities, and entire societies. By examining the correlation between family structure and societal well-being, the mental health implications of rejecting traditional norms, and the empirical evidence supporting the benefits of stable families, we gain a deeper understanding of the challenges posed by modern social changes. While proponents of alternative family structures and fluid identities argue for inclusivity and self-expression, the evidence suggests that adherence to natural norms remains essential for promoting societal health and individual flourishing. In a world increasingly defined by rapid social change, the principles of natural law offer a timeless framework for navigating the complexities of human life and preserving the bonds that hold society together.

Chapter 7

LGBTQ and the Crisis of Identity

Identity Formation and Human Psychology

Identity formation is a critical aspect of human development, shaped by a complex interplay of biological, social, and cultural influences. The process of understanding who we are and how we fit into society requires stability, coherence, and a sense of purpose. Classical and modern psychological theories have emphasized the importance of a coherent sense of self for achieving psychological well-being and social integration.

Erik Erikson, a key figure in developmental psychology, described adolescence as a crucial period for identity exploration and solidification. He wrote, "In the social jungle of human existence, there is no feeling of being alive without a sense of identity" (*Identity: Youth and Crisis*, 1968, p. 109). For Erikson, achieving a stable identity is essential for navigating life's challenges and forming meaningful relationships. When this process is disrupted or prolonged, individuals may experience confusion, anxiety, and a lack of direction.

The LGBTQ movement's emphasis on self-determined and fluid identities presents a challenge to traditional notions of identity formation. While this approach can empower individuals who feel constrained by societal norms, it also raises important questions about the psychological impact of constantly shifting or self-defined identities. Philosopher Charles Taylor has observed that "the modern self is defined by the ability to create and recreate its identity, but this process, when detached from stable norms, can lead to a sense of alienation and insecurity" (*Sources of the Self*, p. 185).

Basing Identity on Objective vs. Subjective Factors

The debate over whether identity should be based on objective or subjective factors is central to the discourse surrounding LGBTQ identities. Traditional perspectives rooted in natural law argue that human identity is grounded in objective realities, such as biological sex, social roles, and moral principles. Thomas Aquinas stated that "actions are morally ordered to an end which is objectively discernible by reason" (*Summa Theologica*, I-II, Q. 1, Art. 3). In this view, identity is not a matter of personal choice or subjective self-definition but is shaped by one's nature and purpose. Basing identity on objective realities provides a stable foundation for self-concept, well-being, and social cohesion.

Conversely, the LGBTQ movement emphasizes subjective self-determination, asserting that individuals have the right to define their own identities regardless of biological or social constraints. This perspective aligns with postmodern critiques of fixed categories and the embrace of fluidity. While it may promote individual autonomy and freedom, it also poses challenges for societal stability. A constantly shifting sense of identity can lead to confusion, undermine social norms, and create a lack of direction for individuals navigating complex social roles.

This brings us to a critical question: If the choice of a certain orientation creates identity, then has society lost its direction? There are countless orientations and identities that can be invented. Shall we now start creating new identities and forming minority groups for every conceivable orientation until all we have is a majority of minority groups? Such an approach risks fragmenting society into competing factions, each demanding recognition and accommodation. The pursuit of endless self-defined identities can lead to a breakdown of common values and a sense of social cohesion.

Existential Crises and Modern Challenges

The emphasis on fluid and self-defined identities contributes to a broader existential crisis in modern society. Rapid social change, the erosion of traditional norms, and the rise of individualism have created a cultural environment in which many people struggle with questions of purpose, meaning, and belonging. Existentialist philosophers such as Jean-Paul Sartre and Viktor Frankl have explored the human search for meaning in a world that often appears chaotic and devoid of inherent purpose.

Sartre argued that "existence precedes essence," meaning that individuals must create their own meaning and identity through their choices and actions (*Existentialism is a Humanism*, p. 29). While this perspective emphasizes personal freedom, it also places a heavy burden on individuals to define themselves in the absence of stable norms. Viktor Frankl, by contrast, believed that meaning could be found through commitment to values and purposeful action. He wrote, "Man's search for meaning is the primary motivation of his life, and it is through meaning that he finds his place in the world" (*Man's Search for Meaning*, p. 121).

The rejection of traditional gender roles and norms may liberate some individuals but can also lead to confusion and uncertainty about one's place in society. The emphasis on self-determined identities, detached from stable norms and values, can create a sense of dislocation and alienation. The pursuit of endless identities, each with its own demands and expectations, risks creating a fractured society in which individuals are defined primarily by their differences rather than their shared humanity.

Linking Identity Debates to Broader Societal Struggles

The crisis of identity is not limited to individuals; it reflects broader societal struggles, including the erosion of community bonds, the rise of political polarization, and the decline of shared moral values. Identity politics, which emphasizes the unique experiences and perspectives of marginalized groups, has become a dominant force in contemporary discourse. While it can empower individuals and promote social justice, it can also exacerbate divisions and create a climate of competition and resentment.

Philosopher Alasdair MacIntyre has argued that the modern world is characterized by "moral fragmentation," in which individuals pursue competing and often incompatible visions of the good (*After Virtue*, p. 205). This fragmentation is evident in debates over identity, where traditional norms clash with contemporary demands for recognition and validation. By rejecting shared norms and objective criteria for identity formation, society risks becoming increasingly fragmented and unable to find common ground.

Conclusion

The crisis of identity in the modern world, exemplified by debates over LGBTQ identities, reflects a deeper struggle over the nature of self, meaning, and social cohesion. While the pursuit of individual freedom and self-expression is important, it must be balanced with the need for stable norms and shared values that promote societal cohesion and individual well-being. The challenge lies in navigating these complex issues in a way that respects individual dignity while preserving the bonds that hold communities together. Through thoughtful dialogue, reasoned debate, and a commitment to common values, society can address the crisis of identity and work toward a more cohesive and inclusive future.

Chapter 8

The Suspicious Weaponization of LGBTQ in the Global South

Cultural Imperialism and LGBTQ Advocacy

The promotion of LGBTQ rights in the Global South has often been perceived as a form of cultural imperialism, where Western nations and international organizations impose their values and norms on societies with deeply rooted traditional beliefs. The exportation of LGBTQ advocacy to regions like Africa, Asia, and the Middle East raises important questions about cultural sovereignty, ethical engagement, and the legitimacy of imposing external moral frameworks on diverse cultures. Uganda, as one of the latest examples, has found itself at the center of this cultural clash, highlighting the tensions between traditional values and external pressures.

Cultural imperialism refers to the practice of imposing one culture's values and beliefs on another, often under the guise of progress or human rights. Frantz Fanon, a prominent postcolonial thinker, warned against the dangers of cultural domination, stating that "the colonial world is a compartmentalized world... In a sense, it becomes a world divided into compartments, hostile to one another" (*The Wretched of the Earth*, p. 37). The imposition of Western LGBTQ norms on societies in the Global South can be seen as a continuation of this historical pattern, where the cultural values of powerful nations are promoted at the expense of indigenous traditions.

In Uganda, the tension between traditional values and Western LGBTQ advocacy has been particularly pronounced. Uganda's cultural and religious leaders have long emphasized the importance of family, community, and moral norms rooted in local customs and religious teachings. The introduction of LGBTQ rights, often accompanied by

Western diplomatic and financial pressure, is perceived by many as an attack on these values. The Ugandan government's enactment of anti-LGBTQ legislation reflects a broader resistance to what is viewed as cultural imperialism. Critics of this approach argue that the imposition of Western norms undermines Uganda's sovereignty and disregards the unique moral and cultural context of the country.

NGOs and Conditional Aid

International aid has historically played a significant role in shaping the policies and cultural norms of recipient countries. In recent years, Western governments and international non-governmental organizations (NGOs) have increasingly tied aid to the acceptance of LGBTQ rights, creating a form of economic coercion that has been met with resistance in the Global South. The practice of using conditional aid to promote LGBTQ acceptance raises ethical concerns about the role of external actors in shaping domestic policies and cultural norms.

Western governments and NGOs often frame their efforts as necessary for the promotion of human rights and social justice. However, critics argue that the use of conditional aid to enforce LGBTQ-friendly policies amounts to a form of economic blackmail that undermines the cultural and moral values of recipient countries. Ugandan leaders, for example, have accused Western nations of using financial leverage to force the country to adopt policies that are contrary to its cultural and religious beliefs. This practice has been described by Ugandan officials as a form of "neo-colonialism," where Western powers seek to impose their moral framework on other societies under the guise of progress.

Philosopher Kwame Anthony Appiah has critiqued the imposition of external norms on diverse cultures, emphasizing the importance of respecting cultural diversity and local autonomy. He writes, "Cultural practices and norms are deeply embedded in the historical and social contexts of societies. Imposing external norms risks erasing these contexts and replacing them with a homogenized, Western-centered morality" (*The Ethics of Identity*, p. 113). The use of conditional aid to promote LGBTQ rights exemplifies this tension, as it disregards the cultural and moral values of recipient countries in favor of a universalized Western agenda.

Resistance and Preservation of Traditional Values

In response to the perceived imposition of Western LGBTQ norms, many countries in the Global South have sought to preserve their traditional values and resist external pressure. This resistance often takes the form of legislative measures, public campaigns, and cultural initiatives aimed at reaffirming local norms and values. Uganda's enactment of anti-LGBTQ laws is one example of this broader resistance, reflecting a determination to defend cultural and moral traditions in the face of external influence.

Traditional values in Uganda and other countries in the Global South are deeply rooted in religious teachings, communal norms, and cultural practices. These values often emphasize the importance of family, community cohesion, and adherence to moral codes that have been passed down through generations. The promotion of LGBTQ rights, which challenges traditional notions of gender and sexuality, is seen by many as a direct threat to these values. Religious leaders, community elders, and political figures have played a central role in resisting the spread of Western LGBTQ norms, framing their efforts as a defense of cultural sovereignty and moral integrity.

Philosopher Edmund Burke, a critic of rapid social change and advocate for tradition, argued that "society is a contract... a partnership not only between those who are living but between those who are dead and those who are to be born" (*Reflections on the Revolution in France*, p. 84). For many in the Global South, the preservation of traditional values is not merely a matter of cultural pride but a moral obligation to maintain continuity and stability for future generations.

Uganda as a Case Study

Uganda's recent experiences illustrate the broader dynamics of resistance and cultural preservation in the face of external pressure. Western governments and NGOs have been vocal in their criticism of Uganda's anti-LGBTQ laws, threatening to withdraw aid and impose diplomatic sanctions. However, many Ugandans view these actions as an attack on their cultural and religious values, reinforcing their determination to resist external influence. The Ugandan government's stance reflects a broader sentiment in the Global South that the promotion of LGBTQ rights must be balanced with respect for cultural and moral traditions.

The debate over LGBTQ rights in Uganda highlights the complexities of cultural exchange, the limits of external influence, and the challenges of navigating conflicting moral frameworks. While proponents of LGBTQ advocacy argue for the universality of human rights, critics emphasize the importance of cultural context and the need to respect diverse moral traditions. The tension between these perspectives underscores the difficulties of promoting social change in a globalized world, where values, norms, and identities are often contested.

Conclusion

The promotion of LGBTQ rights in the Global South raises important questions about cultural imperialism, the use of conditional aid, and the preservation of traditional values. By examining these dynamics, we gain a deeper understanding of the challenges facing societies that seek to navigate the complexities of modernity while preserving their cultural and moral heritage. The resistance to external pressure, exemplified by

Uganda's stance, reflects a broader determination to defend cultural sovereignty and maintain the values that have sustained communities for generations. As the global debate over LGBTQ rights continues, it is essential to engage in thoughtful dialogue that respects the diversity of human cultures and the unique moral frameworks that shape them.

Chapter 9

The Importance of Open Dialogue for Humanity's Survival

Value of Free Speech and Debate

Free speech and open dialogue form the bedrock of any thriving society, enabling the exploration of diverse ideas, challenging entrenched norms, and fostering mutual understanding. The importance of open discourse on controversial issues cannot be overstated; it is essential for the pursuit of truth, social cohesion, and collective progress. Throughout history, philosophers have emphasized the dangers of suppressing dissent, recognizing that stifling alternative viewpoints leads to intellectual stagnation, social unrest, and the consolidation of unchecked power.

John Stuart Mill, a staunch advocate for free expression, argued that "the peculiar evil of silencing the expression of an opinion is that it robs the human race... If the opinion is right, they are deprived of the opportunity of exchanging error for truth; if wrong, they lose, what is almost as great a benefit, the clearer perception and livelier impression of truth, produced by its collision with error" (*On Liberty*, Chapter 2). Mill's argument underscores the critical importance of engaging with differing viewpoints to strengthen our collective understanding and refine our beliefs. By fostering open dialogue, societies can challenge prevailing assumptions, test the validity of new ideas, and create a robust marketplace of ideas.

The ability to speak freely and engage in meaningful debate is also a safeguard against authoritarianism and the concentration of power. In societies where dissent is suppressed, power becomes centralized and unaccountable, leading to widespread abuses and a lack of transparency. Open discourse allows for the airing of grievances, the questioning of authority, and the development of collective solutions to complex social problems. Without this freedom, societies risk becoming fractured, stagnant, and repressive.

Challenges in Modern Discourse

Despite its acknowledged importance, free speech and open dialogue face significant challenges in the modern era. One of the most prominent challenges is the rise of "cancel culture," which involves the public shaming, ostracism, or professional punishment of individuals who express views that are deemed offensive, controversial, or contrary to prevailing norms. While proponents of cancel culture argue that it serves to hold people accountable, critics contend that it creates a climate of fear and self-censorship that stifles open debate and discourages the expression of diverse perspectives.

Philosopher Hannah Arendt, in her analysis of totalitarianism, warned against the dangers of enforcing ideological conformity and suppressing dissent. In *The Origins of Totalitarianism*, she wrote, "The aim of totalitarian education has never been to instill convictions but to destroy the capacity to form any" (p. 385). Although modern societies may not exhibit the same level of totalitarian control, the effects of cancel culture and social ostracism can create a chilling effect on free expression and critical inquiry. When individuals are afraid to express their views for fear of being "canceled," important conversations and debates are stifled, ultimately undermining societal progress.

Social media has further exacerbated these challenges by creating echo chambers that reinforce existing beliefs and isolate people from opposing viewpoints. Algorithms designed to prioritize content based on user preferences contribute to polarization and ideological entrenchment. Philosopher Marshall McLuhan's observation that "the medium is the message" highlights how communication technologies shape human behavior and social norms (*Understanding Media*, p. 19). In the context of social media, the structure of the platforms themselves often discourages meaningful engagement with differing perspectives and encourages conformity.

Examples of Cultural Imperialism Leading to Conflict

Cultural imperialism, the imposition of one culture's values and beliefs over another's, has historically led to conflict and even war. The imposition of foreign norms often provokes backlash and resistance from indigenous populations, resulting in cultural clashes and, at times, violence. Open dialogue and respect for cultural differences are critical for mitigating these tensions and promoting peaceful coexistence.

Colonization of Africa by European Powers: During the 19th and 20th centuries, European colonial powers imposed their languages, religions, and political systems on African societies, often disregarding existing customs and governance structures. This cultural imposition led to widespread resistance and conflicts, such as the Maji Maji Rebellion (1905-1907) in present-day Tanzania. African populations resisted the oppressive labor systems and cultural domination of German colonial rule, resulting in a brutal crackdown by colonial forces and significant loss of life. The legacy of cultural imperialism continues to impact African societies, contributing to internal conflicts and struggles over national identity.

Western Cultural Norms in the Middle East: Western interventions in the Middle East, often framed as efforts to promote democracy, secular governance, and liberal cultural values, have frequently clashed with deeply rooted religious and cultural traditions. The U.S.-led invasion of Iraq in 2003 serves as a notable example. The dismantling of Iraq's political structures and the imposition of Western-style democracy were met with intense resistance, fueling sectarian violence and the rise of extremist groups. This conflict illustrates how attempts to reshape local cultures through external imposition can lead to long-term unrest and violence.

Cultural Imperialism in Indigenous America: European colonization of the Americas involved the systematic suppression of indigenous cultures and the imposition of European customs, languages, and religions. The forced conversion of indigenous peoples to Christianity, coupled with the suppression of traditional practices, led to resistance movements such as the Pueblo Revolt of 1680. This revolt, led by indigenous Pueblo people, sought to expel Spanish colonizers and reclaim cultural sovereignty. The conflict underscores the devastating impact of cultural imperialism and the resilience of indigenous communities in defending their traditions.

British Colonial Rule in India: During British rule in India, the imposition of Western cultural norms, legal systems, and educational practices often clashed with traditional Indian customs and religious practices. The Indian Rebellion of 1857, fueled in part by resentment toward British attempts to reshape Indian society, exemplifies the resistance to cultural imperialism. British efforts to convert Indians to Christianity and impose Western laws were met with widespread anger, resulting in violent conflict and long-term political consequences.

Modern Cultural Imperialism and LGBTQ Advocacy in the Global South: In recent years, Western governments and NGOs have promoted LGBTQ rights as part of their global human rights agenda. While these efforts have led to progress in some areas, they have also been perceived as cultural imperialism by many societies in the Global South, where traditional values and religious norms often conflict with Western views on gender and sexuality. Uganda's resistance to Western LGBTQ advocacy, including the enactment of anti-LGBTQ laws, reflects broader tensions between cultural sovereignty and external pressure. The use of conditional aid to promote LGBTQ rights has been criticized as economic coercion and a continuation of cultural imperialism, leading to backlash and social tension.

Strategies for Constructive Engagement

To address the challenges posed by cultural imperialism, cancel culture, and the suppression of open dialogue, societies must adopt strategies for fostering respectful and constructive engagement. These strategies involve creating spaces for meaningful debate, promoting mutual respect, and respecting cultural diversity.

Creating Respectful Spaces for Dialogue: Societies must encourage open and respectful dialogue on complex issues, allowing individuals to express their views without fear of retribution or ridicule. The Socratic method, which involves asking questions and engaging in reasoned debate, can serve as a model for fostering thoughtful engagement and challenging assumptions.

Balancing Tolerance with Critical Engagement: True tolerance involves engaging with opposing viewpoints while addressing harmful or extremist ideas through dialogue rather than suppression. Philosopher Karl Popper's paradox of tolerance highlights the need to balance tolerance with the protection of open discourse (*The Open Society and Its Enemies*, Vol. 1, p. 265).

Promoting Cultural Sovereignty and Mutual Respect: It is important to recognize that different cultures have different values and norms. Western societies may embrace certain cultural norms, but imposing these norms on other societies can lead to conflict and resentment. As such, it is essential to respect the cultural sovereignty of other nations and engage in dialogue rather than coercion. If LGBTQ rights are embraced in the West, those societies are free to foster their cultural dynamism, but they should not seek to export their norms to societies that do not welcome them, as this can lead to backlash and undermine genuine progress.

Encouraging Diverse Perspectives in Education: Educational institutions play a crucial role in shaping norms and values. By exposing students to a wide range of perspectives and encouraging critical thinking, schools and universities can foster a culture of open dialogue and mutual respect.

Conclusion

Open dialogue and mutual respect are essential for the survival and progress of humanity. By fostering free speech, addressing the challenges of modern discourse, and promoting strategies for respectful engagement, societies can navigate complex cultural, social, and political issues while preserving the bonds that hold communities together. Effective cultural engagement requires dialogue, understanding, and respect for diverse values, ensuring that all voices are heard and considered in the pursuit of a more inclusive and cohesive world.

Conclusion: A Call to Reclaim Natural Order

Natural Law and Human Rights

The concept of natural rights is rooted in the belief that certain rights are inherent to all human beings by virtue of their humanity and are derived from natural law. These rights are universal, inalienable, and grounded in human dignity, reason, and morality. Influential thinkers such as John Locke and Thomas Aquinas articulated the idea that natural rights are intrinsic to human nature and must be respected and protected by society and governments. Locke argued that "all men are naturally in a state of perfect freedom to order their actions... within the bounds of the law of nature" and that no one ought to harm another in their "life, health, liberty, or possessions" (*Two Treatises of Government*, Book II, Chapter 2).

Natural human rights, therefore, include fundamental freedoms such as the right to life, liberty, property, freedom of speech, and freedom of conscience. These rights form the basis of human dignity and the social contract that binds individuals and communities together. The violation of these rights is a grave injustice that undermines human flourishing and social stability.

However, in practice, natural human rights are often violated by the very actors who claim to defend them. While certain countries and international bodies position themselves as champions of human rights, they sometimes engage in actions that undermine the natural rights of individuals and communities. Paradoxically, these same actors often exhibit an intense focus on promoting LGBTQ rights, framing them as an essential component of human rights, even as other fundamental rights are neglected or violated.

Violations of Natural Human Rights by Global Powers

Inconsistent Application of Human Rights Standards: Many Western countries that position themselves as global leaders in human rights have been criticized for selectively applying human rights standards based on political, economic, or strategic interests. For example, while championing LGBTQ rights on the global stage, these same countries may support or turn a blind eye to human rights abuses committed by allied governments. This inconsistency undermines their credibility as human rights advocates and raises questions about the sincerity of their commitment to natural rights.

1. **Example**: The U.S. government has been criticized for supporting authoritarian regimes that engage in human rights abuses, such as suppression of free speech, political dissent, and religious freedom, while simultaneously promoting LGBTQ rights in international forums. This selective approach can be perceived as hypocritical and indicative of a broader agenda that prioritizes certain rights over others based on political expediency.

Violation of Basic Freedoms: In many parts of the world, fundamental human rights such as freedom of speech, freedom of assembly, and the right to life are under threat. Governments and international bodies that claim to uphold human rights sometimes fail to protect these basic freedoms, focusing instead on promoting social and cultural norms that align with their political agenda. This selective approach to human rights advocacy can be seen as a form of cultural imperialism that imposes certain values while disregarding the lived experiences and priorities of local communities.

1. **Example**: In some cases, Western governments have pressured countries in the Global South to adopt LGBTQ-friendly policies as a condition for receiving foreign aid, while remaining silent on other pressing human rights issues, such as poverty, political repression, or human trafficking. This focus on LGBTQ rights, while neglecting broader human rights concerns, has been perceived as an imposition of foreign values and a failure to address the most pressing needs of local populations.

Suppression of Free Speech in the Name of Tolerance: In many Western societies, individuals who express views critical of LGBTQ ideology or advocate for traditional values are often subject to social ostracism, professional consequences, or legal sanctions. This suppression of free speech undermines the natural right to freedom of expression and creates a climate of fear and conformity. Philosopher John Stuart Mill warned against the dangers of silencing dissent, stating that "the peculiar evil of silencing the expression of an opinion is that it robs the human race" of the opportunity to engage with differing perspectives and refine its understanding of truth (*On Liberty*, Chapter 2).

Prioritization of LGBTQ Rights Over Natural Human Rights

While LGBTQ rights advocacy is framed as a human rights issue, critics argue that the intense focus on promoting LGBTQ norms often comes at the expense of addressing more fundamental human rights concerns. The prioritization of LGBTQ rights, particularly in international diplomacy and aid, can create resentment and resistance in societies where traditional norms and values are deeply rooted. This approach can also lead to accusations of cultural imperialism, as external actors impose their values on other cultures while neglecting the broader human rights challenges faced by local populations.

The disproportionate emphasis on LGBTQ rights by some global powers raises important questions about the purpose and priorities of human rights advocacy. If natural human rights, such as the right to life, freedom of speech, and religious freedom, are routinely violated or neglected, why is there such intense focus on promoting LGBTQ norms? Critics argue that this focus reflects a political agenda that seeks to reshape cultural norms and values, rather than a genuine commitment to the universal protection of human rights.

The Need for a Balanced Approach

To protect and promote natural human rights, global society must adopt a balanced approach that respects cultural diversity, upholds fundamental freedoms, and recognizes the unique needs and priorities of different communities. This approach involves:

> **Respecting Cultural Sovereignty**: The imposition of foreign values, including those related to gender and sexuality, must be balanced with respect for the cultural and moral frameworks of different societies. While promoting human rights is important, it should not come at the cost of cultural imperialism or the erosion of local traditions. Philosopher Kwame Anthony Appiah emphasizes the importance of respecting cultural diversity and avoiding the imposition of homogenized, Western-centered norms (*The Ethics of Identity*, p. 113).

Focusing on Universal Human Rights: Efforts to promote LGBTQ rights should not overshadow the broader goal of protecting natural human rights, including the right to life, freedom of speech, and freedom of conscience. A genuine commitment to human rights requires addressing the full spectrum of human rights concerns and engaging with local communities to understand their unique needs and priorities.

Promoting Open Dialogue: Societies must foster open dialogue on complex issues, allowing for respectful debate and the exchange of diverse perspectives. Suppressing dissent or imposing ideological conformity undermines the natural right to freedom of expression and creates a climate of fear and division.

Conclusion: A Vision for the Future

A society rooted in natural law and committed to protecting natural human rights must prioritize fundamental freedoms, respect cultural diversity, and engage in open dialogue. By balancing the promotion of human rights with respect for cultural traditions and the unique needs of different communities, global society can build a future that honors human dignity, promotes well-being, and fosters mutual respect. The intense focus on LGBTQ rights should not come at the expense of other fundamental human rights. Instead, all rights must be protected and promoted in a manner that respects human nature, cultural sovereignty, and the bonds that hold communities together. Through mutual understanding and thoughtful engagement, humanity can navigate the complexities of modern life while preserving the values that sustain social harmony and human flourishing.

Chapter 10

Deep Soul-Searching Questions

Philosophical Consistency

- **Question**: If we argue for the freedom to define personal identity and morality in all aspects of life, should this not logically extend to every person defining their own sense of gender, including those who might identify as animals, machines, or inanimate objects? How do we distinguish the validity of these self-identifications from those who advocate for gender fluidity or non-binary identities?
    - *Reflection*: This question challenges the boundaries of personal identity, urging reflection on where lines should be drawn, if at all, and what philosophical criteria we use to distinguish valid self-identification from purely subjective claims.

Moral Absolutes vs. Relativism

- **Question**: If moral values are entirely relative and subjective, then what grounds do we have for condemning harmful practices like pedophilia or polygamy, which are considered immoral in many societies? Can we, in a purely relativistic framework, claim that one form of human relationship is inherently superior or more ethical than another?
    - *Reflection*: This question probes the tension between moral relativism and universally accepted ethical norms, prompting consideration of whether a purely relativistic approach can sustain a coherent moral framework.

Biological Science

- **Question**: Given that biological sex is determined by DNA and the reproductive system (XX for females and XY for males), how can someone assert that biological sex is fluid, if the foundational science is so clear-cut? How does this affect the legitimacy of any claims about "changing" one's sex, especially in light of the role that sex plays in reproduction?
    - *Reflection*: This question delves into the relationship between biology and gender identity, questioning how claims of fluidity align with established scientific understanding and what implications this has for societal norms.

The Paradox of "Identity"

- **Question**: If gender identity is an entirely social construct, as some argue, what happens to the very concept of "identity" when we allow every individual to self-create it without any external validation? Does this not undermine the entire concept of identity itself by making it arbitrarily changeable and devoid of any intrinsic meaning?
    - *Reflection*: This question raises concerns about the coherence and stability of identity when it is entirely self-defined, prompting reflection on the implications for personal and social integrity.

Scientific and Social Impact

- **Question**: If modern science recognizes that human beings are binary in their sexual reproduction, what societal consequences follow when we promote a model that not only encourages the disconnection of sex from reproduction but also undermines the biological foundation of the family structure? How does this fit with the long-term sustainability of society?
    - *Reflection*: This question explores the potential long-term societal impacts of decoupling sex from reproduction and challenges

proponents of fluid gender models to consider their implications for family and societal stability.

Ethical Boundaries in Medical Science

- **Question**: Is it ethical for medical professionals to assist in gender transitions through surgeries and hormone treatments, especially when we consider the long-term risks and the fact that the individuals undergoing these procedures may be in a vulnerable state of psychological or emotional turmoil? Shouldn't the principle of "do no harm" take precedence?
    - *Reflection*: This question probes the ethics of medical interventions for gender transitions, highlighting the need to balance compassion and care with a commitment to do no harm.

The Concept of "Informed Consent"

- **Question**: When young people, often influenced by social media and peer pressure, transition genders at an early age, do they fully understand the irreversible consequences of such decisions? Should there be an age of maturity, as there is for voting or drinking, before making life-altering decisions regarding one's biological sex?
    - *Reflection*: This question examines the adequacy of informed consent for minors undergoing gender transitions, raising ethical concerns about maturity, understanding, and long-term consequences.

Collective Rights vs. Individual Freedom

- **Question**: How do we reconcile the right of individuals to express their gender identity with the collective rights of society to preserve traditional norms, especially in contexts like education or public policy? Should there be any societal boundaries, or should we allow unrestricted freedom in the name of individual expression?

  - *Reflection*: This question challenges the balance between individual rights and collective societal norms, prompting reflection on where boundaries should be set, if at all.

The Impact on Women's Rights

- **Question**: In a society where gender identity can be self-declared, how do we protect the rights of biological women, especially in areas like sports, single-sex spaces, and healthcare, where the distinction between male and female is important for fairness and safety? Does the promotion of gender fluidity inadvertently harm the very group it aims to empower?
  - *Reflection*: This question highlights potential conflicts between gender fluidity and women's rights, raising concerns about fairness, safety, and the unintended consequences of policy changes.

The Role of Nature in Human Identity

- **Question**: If nature (in the form of biology) has designed humans to be sexually dimorphic, what does it mean for the structure of society and family when this natural order is disregarded? Can human society thrive in a world where natural distinctions are blurred in the name of subjective desires?
  - *Reflection*: This question invites reflection on the role of natural distinctions in human identity and societal order, considering the consequences of disregarding biological realities.

Broader Implications

These questions, grounded in biological science, philosophy, and ethics, are designed to stimulate deep reflection and meaningful dialogue on the underlying assumptions, implications, and potential consequences of LGBTQ advocacy, especially when it is perceived as being weaponized to advance political or cultural agendas. By exploring these issues, individuals and societies can engage thoughtfully with complex questions about identity, morality, and social cohesion, seeking to balance individual rights with collective well-being.

Must We Not Legislate Morality Anymore?

The question of whether we can or should legislate morality is a complex and deeply debated issue that touches on the interplay between law, ethics, and individual freedoms. Morality refers to principles of right and wrong, often shaped by cultural, religious, and philosophical norms, while legislation is the process of creating and enforcing laws that govern society. In many cases, laws are created to reflect and uphold certain moral standards, especially in areas such as criminal justice, where acts like theft, murder, or fraud are prohibited because they are widely considered immoral and harmful to society.

The Argument for Legislating Morality

On one hand, proponents of legislating morality argue that laws serve to promote ethical behavior, protect societal values, and foster a sense of justice and order. By codifying moral principles into law, societies can set clear boundaries for acceptable behavior, safeguard vulnerable populations, and maintain social cohesion. For example, laws against discrimination, hate speech, or environmental harm can be seen as efforts to uphold moral standards that prioritize equality, human dignity, and the protection of the environment.

Philosopher John Locke argued that the role of government is to protect "life, liberty, and property," which are natural rights that reflect fundamental moral principles (*Two Treatises of Government*, Book II). Laws against violence, theft, and fraud, for instance, are grounded in the moral imperative to protect individual rights and promote the common good. In this sense, legislating morality is seen as necessary to ensure justice, fairness, and the well-being of society.

The Argument Against Legislating Morality

On the other hand, critics argue that morality is deeply personal and subjective, shaped by individual beliefs, cultural norms, and religious traditions. Attempts to legislate morality can therefore lead to the imposition of a singular worldview, infringing upon personal freedoms and undermining the diversity of beliefs within a pluralistic society. Laws that seek to regulate personal conduct in areas such as sexual behavior, religious practices, or lifestyle choices are often viewed as overreach by those who believe in the separation of personal morality from state authority.

Philosopher John Stuart Mill, in his work *On Liberty*, emphasized the importance of individual autonomy and warned against the tyranny of the majority imposing its moral values on others. He wrote, "The only purpose for which power can be rightfully exercised over any member of a civilized community, against his will, is to prevent harm to others" (Chapter 1). Mill's "harm principle" suggests that the state should only intervene in matters of personal conduct when an individual's actions harm others. This perspective challenges the notion of legislating morality in areas that do not directly affect the rights or well-being of others.

Balancing Justice and Personal Autonomy

The challenge of legislating morality lies in finding a balance between promoting justice and respecting personal autonomy. While laws may reflect certain moral values, the state must be cautious not to overstep its authority by imposing moral beliefs that infringe on individual freedoms. In some cases, societal consensus can guide the creation of laws that reflect widely accepted moral norms, such as prohibitions against violence or theft. In other cases, efforts to legislate morality may lead to contentious debates and divisions, particularly when laws attempt to regulate personal behavior that does not directly harm others.

For example, debates over laws related to LGBTQ rights, religious practices, or lifestyle choices often highlight the tension between upholding moral standards and respecting personal autonomy. Some argue that laws should reflect traditional moral values to promote social order and cohesion, while others contend that individuals should have the freedom to make their own moral decisions without state interference.

The Role of Morality in Modern Legislation

In modern democratic societies, the role of morality in legislation remains a contentious and evolving issue. Laws that seek to promote ethical behavior and protect vulnerable populations must be carefully crafted to respect individual rights and cultural diversity. Efforts to legislate morality must be grounded in a commitment to justice, fairness, and the common good, while recognizing the limits of state authority in matters of personal morality.

Ultimately, the question of whether and how to legislate morality is one that requires thoughtful deliberation, open dialogue, and a respect for both individual autonomy and the collective values that bind societies together. It is a delicate balance that demands a nuanced understanding of the role of law, ethics, and personal freedom in shaping the moral fabric of society.

Bibliography

Classical Texts:

- Aristotle. *Politics*. Translated works and discussions on the nature of family and society.
- Aristotle. *Metaphysics*. Exploration of the essence and nature of beings.
- Cicero. *De Legibus* (On the Laws). Examination of natural law and morality.
- Cicero. *De Republica* (The Republic). Discussion on customs, laws, and governance.
- Aquinas, Thomas. *Summa Theologica*. Detailed discussions on natural law, human behavior, and moral order.

Modern Studies:

- Appiah, Kwame Anthony. *The Ethics of Identity*. Examination of cultural diversity and identity.
- Dewey, John. *Democracy and Education*. Discussions on education, social norms, and democracy.
- Frankl, Viktor. *Man's Search for Meaning*. Exploration of purpose and meaning in human life.
- Habermas, Jürgen. *The Theory of Communicative Action*. Analysis of public deliberation and communicative action.
- King, M. et al. "Mental Health of LGBTQ Youth." *JAMA Pediatrics*, 2020. Study on mental health challenges.
- MacIntyre, Alasdair. *After Virtue*. Critique of modern moral fragmentation.
- McLanahan, Sara, and Sandefur, Gary. *Growing Up with a Single Parent: What Hurts, What Helps*. Study on family structure and child outcomes.
- Mill, John Stuart. *On Liberty*. Advocacy for free speech and open debate.

- Popper, Karl. *The Open Society and Its Enemies*. Analysis of tolerance and open discourse.
- Scruton, Roger. *Fools, Frauds and Firebrands: Thinkers of the New Left*. Critique of modern social movements.

Historical and Legal Documents:

- Justinian Code. Roman legal texts on morality and behavior.
- National Longitudinal Survey of Youth (NLSY). Data on family stability and societal impacts.
- British Colonial Laws in Uganda. Examination of colonial-era laws on homosexuality and societal norms.
- Historical records on colonial rule and cultural practices in Africa, India, and indigenous America.

Don't miss out!

Visit the website below and you can sign up to receive emails whenever Kayumba David publishes a new book. There's no charge and no obligation.

https://books2read.com/r/B-A-KRSOC-CEKIF

Did you love *LGBTQ Debunked by Natural Law*? Then you should read *Bridging the Rift: A Pacifist Vision for the Israel-Palestine Future*[1] by Kayumba David!

[2]

This book envisions a way forward through a unique confederation model—a path not dependent on dominance but on coexistence, not on division but on shared governance. This confederation is a structure that respects the autonomy and self-determination of each community while fostering cooperation on shared issues. It allows both Israel and Palestine to maintain their own governance, culture, and identity, yet provides a framework through which they can work together as neighbors, partners, and ultimately, as a shared community.

In a world that has seen enough of war and division, a new chapter of humility and hope is required. True peace, as pacifist theologian Stanley

1. https://books2read.com/u/bxk81d

2. https://books2read.com/u/bxk81d

Hauerwas reminds us, is not merely the absence of conflict but the presence of justice, respect, and mutual understanding. Hauerwas writes, "The work of peace is nothing less than the work of worship." Peace is not a passive state but an active practice, a deliberate commitment to see and honor each other as human beings made in the image of God. It requires humility to set aside pride and past grievances, and it demands courage to extend a hand rather than a fist.

Read more at www.zcews.org.

About the Author

Kayumba David is an accomplished author known for his works that span across themes of spirituality, African experiences, and healthcare chaplaincy. His writings often delve into profound social, political, and personal subjects.

One of his notable works is "Visas: The Irony of Freedom", where he critiques the paradoxes faced by many Africans regarding international travel and freedom

He also authored "Hope and Healing: A Chaplain's Handbook," which reflects on his experiences as a chaplain and emphasizes the importance of compassion and spiritual care in healthcare and prison environments

Kayumba's works reflect his personal journey through theological study and lay ministry, having faced challenges within religious institutions, especially during his time in Belgium, where he became an advocate for open theological debate

His contributions in literature offer insights into African realities, the complexities of modern spirituality, and the role of chaplaincy in emotional healing.

Read more at www.zcews.org.

www.ingramcontent.com/pod-product-compliance
Lightning Source LLC
LaVergne TN
LVHW091120150826
845673LV00002B/902

* 9 7 9 8 2 3 0 1 9 3 8 5 2 *